# FLOWERS BY NUMBER

# FLOWERS
# BY
# NUMBER

## WRITTEN BY DAVID SHAPIRO
## ILLUSTRATED BY HAYLEY VAIR

ISBN: 9780984442287

Art Director: Erica Melville
Cover and interior design by Brian David Smith

Printed in the United States of America

2900 SE Stark Street, Suite 1A
Portland, OR 97214
www.craigmorecreations.com

# TO MOM

-David

# 0

# ZERO FLOWERS

It is the middle of winter and a blanket of snow covers the land. There are ZERO flowers out for now.

# 1

# SKUNK CABBAGE

ONE yellow flag of skunk cabbage
announces the arrival of spring in the bog.

*Lysichiton americanus*

# 2
# TWINFLOWER

In the north woods and mountain forests,
TWO twinflowers grow from the same stalk.

*Linnaea borealis*

# 3

## TRILLIUM

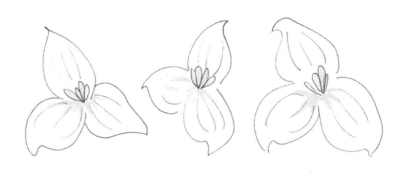

Count THREE trillium and their plant parts.
Three petals, three bracts, three leaves to each
plant, even their name is based on THREE.

*Trillium ovatum*

# 4

# PRICKLY PEAR CACTUS

FOUR prickly pear cacti bloom together in the desert. You can see them and smell them, but don't get too close, those spines will poke!

*Opuntia engelmannii*

# 5

# SALMONBERRY

In the far west, FIVE salmonberry flowers bloom on a bush growing by a stream. Count the FIVE petals so pretty and pink, the fruits will arrive in a matter of weeks.

*Rubus spectabilis*

# 6

# PACIFIC STARFLOWER

SIX pacific starflowers grow in a moist redwood tree grove. SIX petals to count, they look like stars shining on the ground!

*Trientalis latifolia*

# 7

# WATER LILY

SEVEN water lilies catch the rays of the summer sun.
Their roots dive down below where fish and frogs
make their home.

*Nymphaea oderata*

# 8

## YARROW

EIGHT yarrow stand straight in the field.
Like soldiers of summer, they salute
their General, the Sun.

*Achillea millefolium*

# 9

## LUPINE

NINE lupine bloom on the Great Plains.
Named after the wolf, they howl in purple
when many flower at once.

*Lupinus argenteus*

# 10

## COLUMBIA LILY

TEN Columbia lilies bloom like tiger's orange in the forest light. Find them in early summer by the streamside and mountain slope in the great Northwest.

*Lilium columbianum*

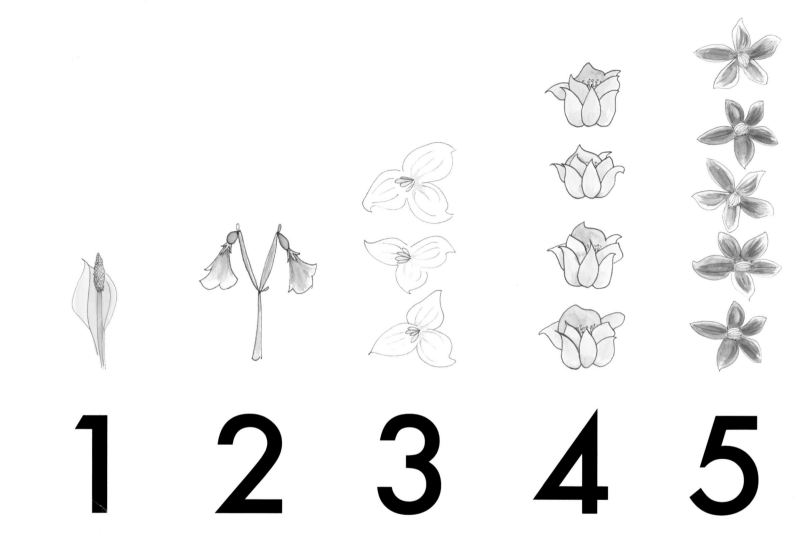

# 1 2 3 4 5

# LET'S COUNT THEM AGAIN!

# 6 7 8 9 10